New York City

New York City

A Downtown America Book

Barbara Johnston Adams

dP Dillon Press, Inc.   Minneapolis, MN 55415

Library of Congress Cataloging-in-Publication Data

Adams, Barbara Johnston.
New York City / by Barbara Johnston Adams.
(A Downtown America book)
Includes index.
Summary: Describes the past and present, boroughs, neighborhoods, historic sites, attractions, and festivals of New York.
ISBN 0-87518-384-0 ,
1. New York (N.Y.)—Juvenile literature.   [1. New York (N.Y.)]
I. Title.   II. Series.
F128.33.A33   1988
974.7'1—dc 19   88-20245
                                               CIP
                                               AC

Dillon Press, Inc., 242 Portland Avenue South
Minneapolis, Minnesota 55415

Printed in the United States of America
1 2 3 4 5 6 7 8 9 10 97 96 95 94 93 92 91 90 89 88

To New York, city of my dreams

Acknowledgments

Special thanks to Charlotte and Robert Johnston, New York Research Center

Photographs have been reproduced through the courtesy of Jim Anderson, Bart Barlow, Jay Dorin, Calvin Finley, the New York Convention and Visitors Bureau, the New York State Department of Commerce, and Joe Viesti.

Contents

Fast Facts about New York City

New York City: The Big Apple

Location: Northeastern United States in the southeastern tip of the state of New York

Area: City, 369 square miles (956 square kilometers); consolidated metropolitan area, 8,249 square miles (21,365 square kilometers)

Population (1986 estimate*): City (all five boroughs), 7,262,700; consolidated metropolitan area, 17,967,800

Major Population Groups: Blacks, Jews, Italians, Puerto Ricans, Irish

Altitude: 55 feet (16.5 meters) above sea level

Climate: Average temperature is 33°F (1°C) in January, 74°F (23°C) in July; average annual precipitation including rain and snow is 44 inches (112 centimeters)

Founding Date: 1625, chartered as a city in 1653

City Flag: The colors of the New York City flag—blue, white, and orange—represent the Dutch flag, and the city seal lies in the flag's center

City Seal: An American eagle, an English sailor, and a Manhattan Indian surround a shield marked with a Dutch windmill, beavers, and barrels

Form of Government: The mayor is elected to a four-year term and is the chief executive of the city government. The city council, which represents the city's thirty-five districts, is the law-making body of the city. The Board of Estimate consists of the council president, the presidents of the five boroughs, the city comptroller, and the mayor. The Board of Estimate advises the mayor as well as the city council.

Important Industries: Printing and publishing, entertainment, advertising, fashion, finance, construction, and communications

*U.S. Bureau of the Census 1988 population estimates available in fall 1989; official 1990 census figures available in 1991-92.

Festivals and Parades

January: Winter Festival (Central Park)

January/February: Chinese New Year

February: Black History Month (American Museum of Natural History)

March: Saint Patrick's Day Parade; Greek Independence Day Parade

March/April: Easter Parade; Easter Egg Rolling Contest (Central Park)

May: Brooklyn Bridge Day; Martin Luther King, Jr. Memorial Day Parade; Ninth Avenue International Festival; Washington Square Outdoor Art Show

June: Kool Jazz Festival; Museum Mile Festival; Puerto Rican Day Parade; Saint Anthony Festival

July: Independence Day celebrations; Our Lady of Mount Carmel Parade (Brooklyn, Bronx); Feast of the Assumption Parade (Bronx)

August: Greenwich Village Jazz Festival; Lincoln Center Out-of-Doors

September: Feast of San Gennaro (Little Italy); "New York is Book Country" (5th Avenue); The 42nd Street Fair; Third Avenue Street Festival

October: Columbus Day Parade; Halloween Parade (Greenwich Village); Pulaski Day Parade

November: Macy's Thanksgiving Day Parade; Radio City Music Hall Christmas Spectacular

December: Hanukkah Celebration, 92nd Street Y (YM/YWHA); Rockefeller Center Tree-Lighting Ceremony; New Year's Eve fireworks over Central Park

For further information about festivals and parades, see agencies listed on page 56.

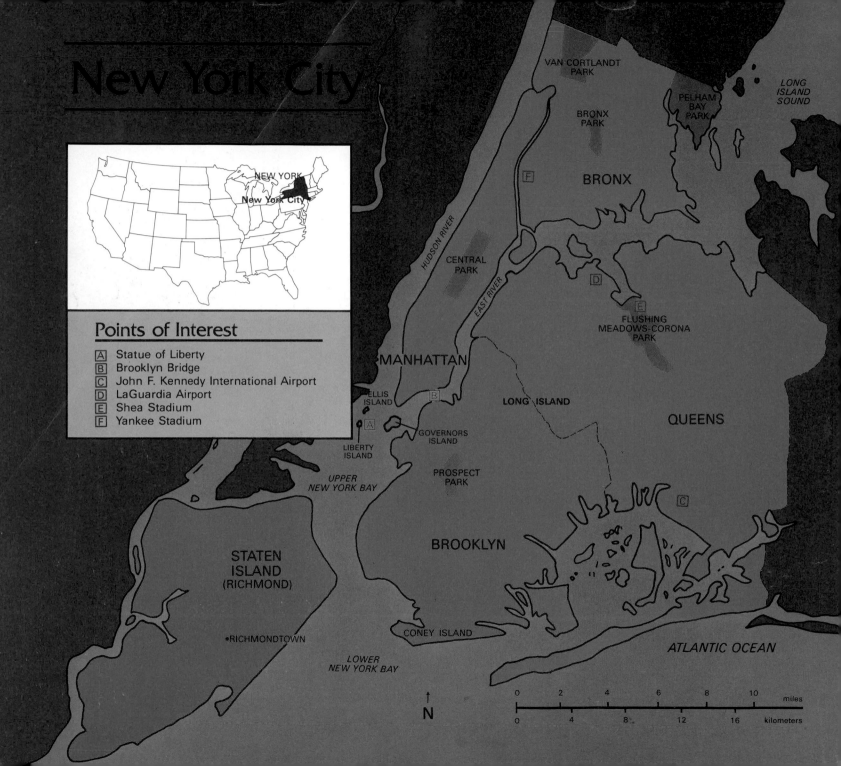

New York City

Points of Interest

- A Statue of Liberty
- B Brooklyn Bridge
- C John F. Kennedy International Airport
- D LaGuardia Airport
- E Shea Stadium
- F Yankee Stadium

NEW YORK

New York City

VAN CORTLANDT PARK

PELHAM BAY PARK

LONG ISLAND SOUND

BRONX PARK

BRONX

F

HUDSON RIVER

CENTRAL PARK

EAST RIVER

D

E

FLUSHING MEADOWS-CORONA PARK

MANHATTAN

ELLIS ISLAND

B

LONG ISLAND

QUEENS

A

GOVERNORS ISLAND

LIBERTY ISLAND

UPPER NEW YORK BAY

PROSPECT PARK

C

STATEN ISLAND (RICHMOND)

BROOKLYN

•RICHMONDTOWN

CONEY ISLAND

ATLANTIC OCEAN

LOWER NEW YORK BAY

N

0		2		4		6		8		10	
											miles
0		4		8		12		16			kilometers

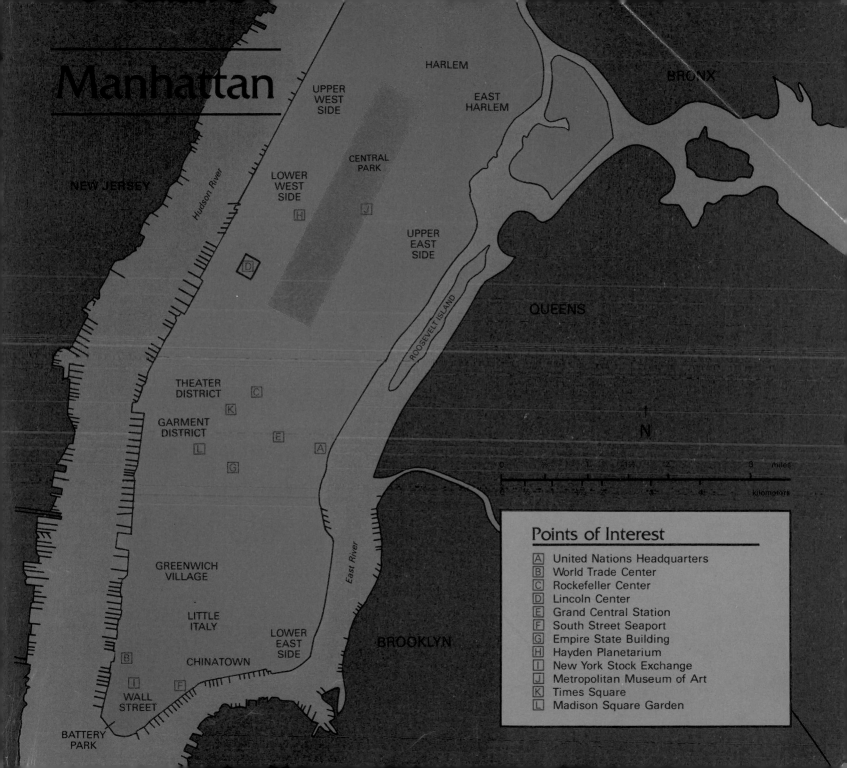

Manhattan

NEW JERSEY

HARLEM

BRONX

EAST
HARLEM

UPPER
WEST
SIDE

Hudson River

LOWER
WEST
SIDE

CENTRAL
PARK

Ⓗ

Ⓙ

Ⓓ

UPPER
EAST
SIDE

QUEENS

ROOSEVELT ISLAND

THEATER
DISTRICT

Ⓒ

Ⓚ

GARMENT
DISTRICT

Ⓔ

Ⓛ

Ⓐ

Ⓖ

↑
N

0   ½   1   1½   2   3   miles

0   ½   1   1½   2   3   4   kilometers

GREENWICH
VILLAGE

East River

LITTLE
ITALY

LOWER
EAST
SIDE

BROOKLYN

CHINATOWN

Ⓑ

Ⓘ   Ⓕ

WALL
STREET

BATTERY
PARK

Points of Interest

Ⓐ United Nations Headquarters
Ⓑ World Trade Center
Ⓒ Rockefeller Center
Ⓓ Lincoln Center
Ⓔ Grand Central Station
Ⓕ South Street Seaport
Ⓖ Empire State Building
Ⓗ Hayden Planetarium
Ⓘ New York Stock Exchange
Ⓙ Metropolitan Museum of Art
Ⓚ Times Square
Ⓛ Madison Square Garden

1

Gateway to America

The "Big Apple"—that's what New York City is called. New Yorkers feel they live in the center of the universe. Everything is faster, higher, and more impressive in New York. This is a city where anything can happen.

Young jazz musicians first called New York the "Big Apple" in the 1920s—the Roaring Twenties—when the U.S. economy was booming, spirits were high, and jazz was popular.

When entertainers said they were going to the "Big Apple," they meant, "I've made it to the top," or "I'm playing the big time!" Young people continue to come to New York—the city is a magnet for anyone with a dream.

New York, above all, is exciting. Never sleeping, the city is in full swing twenty-four hours a day. An adventure lies around every corner. Build-

A view of Manhattan from New York Harbor.

People and traffic rush through the streets of Manhattan.

ings, streets, and parks could change at any moment as the old makes way for the new. The Broadway show that is sold out today may close next month.

Because millions of people visit, live, and work in New York, it's a place where it pays to be careful. Hit-and-run thieves watch for those who forget to hold tightly to purses and wallets. New Yorkers know how to walk and talk to avoid trouble.

The city is crowded, but most New Yorkers have a place to call home. Some of the citizens, however, have nowhere to live. Hungry and homeless people share the city with people who have everything. Wealthy families in expensive homes may live only blocks away from families struggling to keep warm.

Anyone who passes through New York—for a long or short time—learns that the city can be both beautiful and ugly. It can have the best and worst of everything.

The city of New York is one of the largest cities in the United States, and is among the largest cities in the world. Located in New York State, the city has been in the international spotlight from the earliest days of American history.

New York's location made the city an important trade and business center. Mighty rivers flow into a majestic harbor, which empties into the Atlantic Ocean. One of the rivers, the Hudson, is named after the Englishman Henry Hudson, who explored the region for the Dutch in 1609.

Dutch families working for the West India Company were the first Europeans to settle in what is now New York City. In 1664, after years of fighting, the English forced the Dutch to surrender the land. The British settlers named the land New York in honor of the English duke of York.

In the 1700s, the American colonists began to resent the rule of the British, and they were willing to fight for their freedom. The Revolutionary War, which began in 1775 and lasted

until 1783, led to the creation of the United States of America.

New York City was considered the capital of the United States from 1785 to 1790. George Washington, a general in the Revolutionary War, took the oath of office as America's first president in Federal Hall in 1789.

From its founding, New York has served as the gateway to America. Starting in the 1890s, millions of immigrants passed through Ellis Island in New York Harbor. While many immigrants moved on to other cities, some settled in New York. Today, the city still draws people from around the world. One out of every two New Yorkers is either foreign-born or has a parent who came to the city from another country.

The Statue of Liberty, a gift from France to the United States, was restored in 1986, on the Lady's hundredth birthday.

An aerial view of Ellis Island in New York Harbor.

A 151-foot (46-meter) woman is another striking part of New York Harbor. The Statue of Liberty, sometimes called "the Lady," welcomes immigrants to New York's shores.

The boat ride to the statue on Liberty Island offers a chance to see the New York skyline. The view from her crown takes in the bay and different parts of the huge city of New York.

2

The Five (Boroughs) 5
(Buros)

New York City is divided into five sections known as boroughs. Many people think of the island of Manhattan when they think of New York, because the island is considered the "heart of the city." Manhattan is a borough, along with Brooklyn, Queens, the Bronx, and Richmond, or Staten Island.

The boroughs, which are also separate counties, are connected to one another, to other parts of New York State, and to New Jersey by bridges and tunnels. Each has its own character, and the people who live in each part of the city like to boast that theirs is the best.

Brooklynites point out that New York's most famous bridge carries the name of their borough. Completed in 1883, the Brooklyn Bridge spans the East River, which separates Manhat-

The Brooklyn Bridge stretches from Brooklyn to Manhattan.

The Brooklyn Heights neighborhood is well known for its elegant apartment houses.

tan from the western end of Long Island.

Brooklyn has more residents than any other borough, and is also an important port and industrial center. This New York section has many churches, parks, and neighborhoods.

Attractions such as Prospect Park, the Brooklyn Museum, and the Brooklyn Academy of Music draw many people to this part of the city. On hot summer weekends, millions of New Yorkers crowd the beaches at Coney Island.

The Brooklyn Botanic Gardens' many points of interest include three Japanese gardens.

Next to Brooklyn on Long Island, across the East River from Manhattan, is the borough of Queens. One of the area's most popular parks is Flushing Meadows-Corona Park, the site of two World's Fairs. Queens is also known for its huge housing developments and the two major New York City airports: John F. Kennedy (named for America's thirty-fifth president) and LaGuardia (named for a famous New York City mayor). Millions of travelers pass through these airports each year.

Shea Stadium attracts many sports fans to Queens. One of New York's major league baseball teams, the Mets, plays here. Many international tennis matches, including the U.S. Open Tennis Championships, are also played in Queens.

The Bronx is the northernmost borough of New York City. An early land owner, Jonas Bronck, gave his name to part of what is now called the Bronx.

City Island, a Bronx neighborhood, has the smell of salt air in its streets. An actual island on Long Island Sound, it is a center for yacht building and sailing supply stores.

Some parts of the Bronx have run-down housing and dangerous street crime. In the South Bronx area, conditions became so bad that whole blocks of buildings were torn down. Slowly the city is struggling to bring this section back to life.

Large parks such as Van Cortlandt Park, which has woods, fields, and lakes, provide a green escape for Bronx residents. Pelham Bay Park has its own saltwater beach on Long Island Sound. At the borough's center is Bronx Park, which includes the famous Bronx Zoo and the New York Botanical Garden.

The New York Yankees, a major league baseball team, play at the Bronx's Yankee Stadium. The stadium used to feature the New York Giants football team, but now the Giants and the Jets both play in New Jersey.

Shea Stadium, which seats 55,000 people, is located in Queens' Flushing Meadows-Corona Park.

Since Staten Island is across New York Harbor from Manhattan, some people don't realize that it, too, is a borough of the city. With its neatly kept homes, hills and valleys, and wildlife refuge, the island seems far away from the push and shove of Manhattan. The twenty-five-cent ferry boat ride from Staten Island to Manhattan and back again carries commuters to and from work. Richmondtown, located in the middle of the island, is being restored to show its historical development since the 1600s.

Many visitors to New York see only one of the city's boroughs—Manhattan. This small, narrow island is New York City's oldest and most important borough. The Algonquin Indians, who first lived on the island, called it Manhata or Manhatin, which means "Island of the Hills." Peter Minuit, an early Dutch governor, paid the Algonquins about twenty-four dollars worth of trinkets for the entire island of Manhattan!

Manhattan is the center of many of America's industries, and is home to an incredible variety of people. Most races, religions, and national groups have played a part in making Manhattan the booming international center it is today. Places from houses of worship to restaurants reveal the many different traditions that have taken root and thrived here.

The Staten Island Ferry trip provides excellent views of the busy harbor and Manhattan's skyline.

Slices of the Big Apple

Millions of busy people are squeezed into the boundaries of Manhattan Island. When they are tired of city streets and skyscrapers, Central Park provides a welcome taste of nature. Other smaller parks also offer places to relax.

Manhattan has an East Side and a West Side, with Fifth Avenue dividing the two. The East Side lies between Fifth Avenue and the East River, while the West Side covers the area from Fifth Avenue to the Hudson River.

Since there are one and a half million people who live on one small island, housing is a serious problem in Manhattan. In this borough, most people rent the places where they live. Around 200,000 New Yorkers live in city-owned public housing, often in large, high-rise projects. But many

The lower end of Manhattan Island.

In Central Park, New Yorkers can enjoy picnics, row boats, or ride in horse-drawn carriages.

New Yorkers in the other four boroughs own their own homes.

Many different neighborhoods and areas make up New York City. Some of these reflect the immigrants from around the world who settled here. Three-fourths of New York's population includes Irish, Italian, Jewish, Puerto Rican, and black Americans. Polish, German, Greek, and Russian Americans also live in the city, as well as many groups from Asian countries.

Immigrants from China came to

settle in what is now called Manhattan's Chinatown. Within Chinatown and in other parts of Lower Manhattan, thousands of Chinese live in crowded apartment buildings, or tenements.

Walking through Chinatown is like visiting another country. The telephone booths resemble little pagodas, or Asian temples. Along the streets, wind chimes jingle outside of stores, and fresh meats hang in market windows. Foods such as snow peas, bean curd, shark fins, and duck eggs are for sale. In warm weather, the bright colors of fresh fruit and vegetable stands fill the narrow, winding streets.

Chinatown parades celebrate the start of the Chinese New Year. Fire-

Restaurants, markets, and shops line the streets of Chinatown.

crackers explode, and people dressed in costumes dance in the streets. Many other people with Asian backgrounds—Vietnamese, Indian, Korean, Filipino, and Japanese—also celebrate their own traditions throughout the city.

Little Italy is just north of Chinatown. This Manhattan neighborhood has the smells, sounds, and sights of some Italian cities. New Yorkers from other parts of the city come here to enjoy pasta and other Italian dishes. The Festival of San Gennaro draws many visitors to Little Italy. For this festival, a part of Mulberry Street becomes a giant carnival with games and ferris wheel rides. Food stands sell treats such as calzone and zeppola.

The Lower East Side of Manhattan is a "melting pot" of races, religions, and ways of life. In the early 1900s, immigrants lived here crowded together in run-down buildings. Only the strongest people survived the poverty and sickness that spread through the crowded slum. Some escaped to a better life by getting an education in New York's public schools and colleges. Many became famous entertainers, politicians, or business people.

Of those who came to the Lower East Side, many were Jewish. Today, many Jewish stores are still in business here. Sunday is a big shopping day since the stores are closed on Saturday, the Jewish Sabbath. A large number of Puerto Ricans now live in this part of Manhattan.

At the northern part of the island is Harlem, sometimes called the "capital of black America." When the Dutch settlers came to this area, they named it Nieuw Haarlem after a Netherlands town. Harlem's immigrants and their descendants come from many lands, including Cuba, the West Indies, Africa, Puerto Rico, and Haiti. A large Hispanic population lives in East Harlem, also known as Spanish Harlem.

In the 1800s and the early part of this century, handsome brownstone houses, schools, and stores were built in Harlem. Black families began to pour into this section of Manhattan. Harlem boomed as a center of arts and entertainment in the 1920s. Black artists produced new

Some of Harlem's elegant housing is found in the Striver's Row neighborhood.

works of poetry, painting, and music. Famous nightclubs like the Cotton Club offered music by such great performers as Lena Horne, Duke Ellington, and Count Basie. The Apollo Theatre became a showcase for talented black entertainers.

The Harlem Globetrotters first started out in 1927 as an all-black professional basketball team, playing exhibition games across the country. The team is now based in California. The Boys Choir of Harlem is another internationally famous group of Harlem performers.

Over the years, Harlem turned into a slum. Though the area still has many problems, parts of it are reviving. Families are fixing up the old brownstone homes in historic dis-

The corner of 135th and Lenox streets in Harlem.

tricts. Harlem museums and libraries also keep the area's history alive. The Schomburg Center has the largest library of black and African history in the United States. Harlem is known for its large variety of theater companies, dance companies, and museums.

Greenwich (pronounced GRENitch) Village was settled in the late 1700s when people were fleeing from yellow fever in the lower city. More than a century later, the Village attracted painters, sculptors, poets, and playwrights. These artists, struggling to work with little money, found they could rent rooms cheaply in the Village's old, high-ceilinged buildings.

Today, the neighborhood is expensive, and housing rates have forced many of the artists to move. People who can afford the high rents now live in the old Village buildings. On one famous street, MacDougal Alley, houses still have doorways lighted by gas lamps.

The lower part of Manhattan is where the Dutch first settled. The glass and metal skyscrapers that crowd this area make the winding streets seem very narrow. Old New York can still be seen here and there. At one end of Wall Street is Trinity Church, built in 1846. The land for this church was given by Queen Anne of England, and the cemetery next to the church contains graves dating from the 1600s.

Battery Park, at the southern end of Manhattan, also has many histori-

cal landmarks. Castle Clinton isn't a castle, but an old fort, built in 1811 to defend New York from British attack. In time, the fort became a theater, an immigration center, and later an aquarium. Bowling Green, where people really used to bowl, is a stop for many of New York's subway lines.

Since colonial times, the width of Lower Manhattan has almost doubled. Battery Park City, not far from the tip of the island, was built on newly created land. Builders took huge loads of soil and sand and filled up parts of the Hudson River. They used soil from the giant holes that were dug to construct the World Trade Center Towers, and from the sandy bottom of New York Harbor.

Office buildings, apartment houses, and stores stand on this new land, and construction will continue here until the year 2000. Two parts of this community stand out—the Winter Garden, a glass enclosure the size of a football stadium, and a long walkway by the Hudson River with cobblestones and old-fashioned street lights.

Manhattan is an amazing place. This narrow island is more than the bustling center of New York City. In many ways, it is a symbol for all of America.

Battery Park overlooks New York's busy harbor.

The Big Time

New Yorkers have good reason to think their city is important. New York is the U.S. headquarters for fashion, finance, advertising, publishing, and entertainment. People still flock to New York to hit the "big time" in whatever field they are in.

Events in New York affect what happens all over the world. In fact, the United Nations has its headquarters on the banks of Manhattan's East River. The thirty-nine-story Secretariat Building reflects the river in its all-glass walls. More than a million people a year enter the General Assembly Building. They come to see where representatives from U.N. member countries meet to work for world peace. Outside this building fly these nations' colorful flags.

New York affects the world in less obvious ways, too. If people buy

Manhattan at night.

shirts in Florida, the money they spend may, without their realizing it, help support New York's fashion industry. Decisions about the style and fabric of clothing, from jeans to bathing suits, are made in the Garment District on the West Side of Manhattan. Talk is loud and actions are fast in this district. Big racks of clothing are pushed from factory doors to trucks for delivery to stores.

New York is full of elegant stores. Saks Fifth Avenue, Lord & Taylor, Bergdorf Goodman, and B. Altman's are a few of the famous department stores located on Fifth Avenue. Another Fifth Avenue store is F.A.O. Schwartz, a fantastic toy store that sells hundreds of stuffed animals, model trains, full-sized log cab-

Left: The United Nations headquarters. *Right:* Fifth Avenue bustles with activity.

ins, and more. Macy's, a huge department store on Herald Square, is known for sponsoring the Macy's Thanksgiving Day Parade.

Wall Street, located in the center of the Financial District, is home to the New York Stock Exchange. Here, fortunes can be made and lost in a matter of hours. People follow the ups and downs of major companies in the respected *Wall Street Journal*. Another newspaper read throughout the world is the *New York Times*.

When Americans open a newspaper or watch television, they see many advertisements created in New York. The Big Apple has a large number of advertising agencies, many of them located on Manhattan's Madison Avenue.

Macy's Thanksgiving Parade marches down the streets of Manhattan.

The New York Stock Exchange is the largest organized market for stocks and bonds in the United States.

Publishing is also an important New York City industry. Many magazine, book, and video publishers and printers have offices here. Each fall, Fifth Avenue is the scene for a big book fair called "New York is Book Country."

With over sixty radio and television shows, New York is an important communications center. The nation's major television and radio networks, including ABC, CBS, and NBC, are all based in New York. NBC gives tours of its studios, where television programs such as *The Today Show* are filmed. NBC headquarters are in a group of twenty-one buildings called Rockefeller Center, well known for its winter outdoor ice skating rink and summer café.

Scattered throughout the city are places that offer all kinds of entertainment—theater, dance, and music performances. Radio City Music Hall, also located in Rockefeller Center, entertains audiences with films and stage shows. The theater, which seats 6,000 people, often features performances by the high-kicking dancers called the Rockettes.

Of all the plays and musicals that have try-out performances on American stages, only a few make it to the "big time" of New York's theater district. Theaters in this district are located near Times Square and the street known as Broadway. Times Square is nicknamed the "Great White Way" for its bright lights.

In the Upper West Side of Manhattan, Lincoln Center for the Performing Arts provides another special world of entertainment. Lincoln Center includes a concert hall, a performing arts library, an opera house, a dance theater, and other stages for plays. The huge center hosts the New York Philharmonic, the Metropolitan Opera, the New York City Ballet, the New York City Opera, and the Juilliard School of Music.

One of the world's best performing arts centers is New York's Carnegie Hall. The finest orchestras, musicians, and singers have appeared here since the beautiful concert hall first opened in 1891.

New York's entertainment industry attracts and encourages young people with talent. The High School of

The gold statue of Prometheus in front of Rockefeller Center.

Performing Arts, featured in the movie and the television series called "Fame," has now combined with another school to become the Fiorello H. LaGuardia High School of Music and the Arts. Though it is a public school, students must audition, or try out, to enter the school. If they pass this test and are admitted, they will take regular high school subjects as well as courses in their field of interest.

Not all of New York's schools focus on the arts. New York, with over 960 public schools, has the largest public school system in the United States. Two public schools, the Bronx High School of Science and Stuyvesant High, are known for their excellent science programs.

New York has many fine colleges and universities as well. City University of New York is one of the largest universities in the world. Columbia University and New York University are private schools.

For people who want to achieve their dreams of success, or search for an exciting adventure, "big time" New York has much to offer.

Lincoln Center features year-round entertainment in music, theater, and dance.

Around Town

In New York City, there is always somewhere to go and something to do. When New Yorkers want to get someplace, they have many kinds of transportation from which to choose. The method they pick can depend on the time of day and the weather—subways, buses, limousines, taxis, or even roller skates! Bumper-to-bumper traffic often makes walking the best way to go.

New York's subway systems connect with its railroad centers at Grand Central Station and Pennsylvania Station. Grand Central Terminal has been around for more than seventy-five years. Each day at least five hundred trains arrive and leave from the terminal, and half a million people or more walk through its doors.

Another way to get around New York City is by boat. The Staten

Grand Central Station's main room is one of the largest rooms in the world.

A Manhattan street vendor displays his wares at the Fulton Fish Market.

Island Ferry provides a spectacular view of the Manhattan skyline, and the Circle Line boats take a three-hour tour around Manhattan Island.

South Street Seaport, on the East River, is a good place to learn about the city's earlier days as a great shipping center. Square riggers, whaling ships, and even a ship used as a floating lighthouse line the docks. Schermerhorn Row, a series of warehouses built in the 1800s, is now full of shops and restaurants. The nearby Fulton Fish Market processes and sells fish for New York and the surrounding areas.

During the city's peak shipping years, the East River served as the main docking area. Today, most cargo ships dock at other areas of the

Large historic ships dock at the lively South Street Seaport.

New York waterfront and sections of the New Jersey coast.

The Hudson River has docks for cruise ships, many of which sail for vacation spots in faraway places. One passenger liner, the *Queen Elizabeth 2*, crosses the Atlantic Ocean on a regular schedule. Passengers and visitors can stand in a glass-enclosed terminal to watch the ships come and go from the docks.

One famous part of the Manhattan skyline is the Empire State Building. For about forty years, this was

the tallest building in the world. (The Sears Tower, in Chicago, is now the tallest.) Each year, more than a million and a half visitors take the elevator to the observatory high above the city's busy streets.

The tallest buildings in New York today are the twin towers of the World Trade Center. These towers are like vertical cities—about 50,000 people work in them and in connected buildings. The trade center has restaurants, a shopping mall, and offices, as well as the world's highest open-air platform.

Another interesting spot in Manhattan is Madison Square Garden. "The Garden," as many call the 20,000-seat arena, used to be famous for its boxing matches. Now, New

The twin towers of the World Trade Center loom high above Lower Manhattan.

Madison Square Garden.

York's pro-basketball team, the Knickerbockers (the Knicks), and the pro-hockey team, the Rangers, play here. The arena also hosts rock concerts, rodeos, and even the Ringling Brothers Barnum and Bailey Circus.

New York has a number of zoos, and the Bronx Zoo is one of the best in the world. The zoo provides space for the animals to roam around. The "Plains of Africa" are home to gazelle, antelope, and giraffes, while the "Wild Asia" section has tigers and rhinoceroses.

Near the Sixty-fourth Street entrance to Central Park is a zoo known for its sea lions and its playful monkeys. At a smaller zoo in Central Park, the Children's Zoo, the only way an adult can get in is to go with a child.

Coney Island's New York Aquarium features everything from a huge shark tank to a special Children's Cove, where young people can touch starfish and seashells in special boxes. Astroland, a large amusement park, also draws crowds to Coney Island.

Many of New York's museums have exhibits or events especially designed for young people. The Metropolitan Museum of Art contains more than three million pieces of art. The "Met" also has a junior museum with changing exhibits, and sometimes stages gallery hunts where children are sent through the museum with "treasure maps."

The American Museum of Natural History offers dinosaur and meteorite collections. It also displays a life-size whale hanging from the ceiling, and the Star of India, a sapphire the size of a golf ball.

The Hayden Planetarium forms a separate part of the Museum of Natural History. Inside the planetarium is a huge dome onto which tiny pinpricks of light—some made by lasers—are projected. The light beams look like stars and planets. During these spectacular star shows, a narrator explains the universe while changing the beams of light.

Coney Island, a famous seaside resort, features Astroland amusement park, restaurants, arcades, and a skating rink along the boardwalk.

Brooklyn is home to the Brooklyn Museum, known for its collection of ancient Egyptian art. The Brooklyn Children's Museum, built in 1889, offers films, live performances, and many things to touch.

One of New York's museums floats on the water—on a U.S. Navy aircraft carrier. The Intrepid Sea-Air-Space Museum docks at Pier 86 on the Hudson River. Exhibits such as space shuttles, lunar landing modules, and old-fashioned flying machines are spread throughout the ship.

Young people can take a walk into the future at the InfoQuest Center in the AT&T building. Here, visitors can program a robot, direct a music video, and send a message via fiber optics. Right across the street is the IBM Building's Gallery of Science and Art, which provides shows that change several times a year.

Countless other attractions line the streets of New York City. Even for the people who live there, New York is an exciting, challenging, ever-changing city. Its fast pace, unlimited opportunities, and rich mixture of ways of life cause some to say, "You have to be a little crazy to live in New York, but you'd be nuts to live anywhere else."

The aircraft carrier U.S.S. *Intrepid* is now a floating museum.

Places to Visit in New York

AT&T InfoQuest Center
Madison Avenue at 56th Street
(212) 605-5555

American Museum of Natural History
Central Park West at 79th Street
(212) 769-5000

Bronx Zoo
Fordham Road and Bronx River Parkway,
the Bronx
(212) 367-1010

Brooklyn Botanic Garden
Washington Avenue between Eastern Parkway and Empire Boulevard, Brooklyn
(718) 622-4433

Brooklyn Children's Museum
Brooklyn Avenue at St. Mark's Avenue,
Brooklyn
(718) 735-4400

Brooklyn Museum
Eastern Parkway and Washington Avenue,
Brooklyn
(718) 638-5000

Central Park Children's Zoo
5th Avenue and 64th Street
(212) 408-0271

Children's Museum of Manhattan
54th Street between 8th and 9th avenues
(212) 765-5904

Con Edison Energy Museum
14th Street between 3rd Avenue and Irving
Place
(212) 460-6244

Empire State Building
5th Avenue at 34th Street
(212) 736-3100

F.A.O. Schwartz
5th Avenue between 58th and 59th streets
(212) 644-9400

Federal Hall National Memorial
Wall Street at Nassau Street
(212) 264-8711

Grand Central Terminal
42nd Street and Park Avenue
(212) 935-3969 for tour information

Guggenheim Museum
5th Avenue at 88th Street
(212) 360-3500
An ultra-modern, Frank Lloyd Wright-designed museum of modern art

Hayden Planetarium
Central Park West at 81st Street
(212) 769-5920

Hispanic Society of America
Broadway at 155th Street
(212) 690-0743
A library and museum of Hispanic culture

IBM Building/Gallery of Science and Art
Madison Avenue and 56th Street
(212) 407-6100

Intrepid Sea-Air-Space Museum
Pier 86, 46th Street and 12th Avenue
(212) 245-0072

Lincoln Center for the Performing Arts
Between 62nd and 66th streets, west of Broadway
(212) 877-1800

Metropolitan Museum of Art
5th Avenue at 82nd Street
(212) 879-5500

Museum of Modern Art
53rd Street between 5th and 6th avenues
(212) 708-9400

New York Aquarium
Surf Avenue and West 8th Street, Coney Island, Brooklyn
(718) 265-3474

New York Botanical Garden
Southern Boulevard and Pelham Parkway, the Bronx
(212) 220-8700

New York Chinatown History Project
Mulberry Street at Bayard Street
(212) 619-4785

"The New York Experience"
McGraw-Hill Plaza Building
6th Avenue between 48th and 49th streets
(212) 869-0345
Multi-media show about New York's history

New York Hall of Science
111th Street and 48th Avenue, Flushing,
Queens
(718) 699-0005

New York Public Library
5th Avenue at 42nd Street
(212) 869-8089

New York Stock Exchange
Broad Street at Wall Street
(212) 656-5168

Radio City Music Hall
6th Avenue at 50th Street
(212) 246-4600 for backstage tour

Rockefeller Center
5th Avenue between 48th and 51st streets

Schomburg Center for Research in Black
Culture
Lenox Avenue and 135th Street
(212) 862-4000

South Street Seaport
Fulton Street at the East River
(212) 669-9400

Statue of Liberty
Ferry leaves from State Street in Battery
Park to Liberty Island
(212) 363-3200

United Nations
1st Avenue at 46th Street
(212) 963-1234

World Trade Center
2 World Trade Center
Liberty Street between West and Church
streets
(212) 466-7397

Additional information can be obtained
from these agencies:

New York Convention and Visitors Bureau
Two Columbus Circle
New York, NY 10019
(212) 397-8222

New York State Department of Commerce
55 Elk Street
Albany, NY 12245
(518) 474-4116

New York: A Historical Time Line

1524   Giovanni da Verrazano lands on what is now called Staten Island

1609   Henry Hudson sails up what is now called the Hudson River

1624   The colony of New Netherland is established on Manhattan Island

1625   The town of New Amsterdam is established as capital of New Netherland

1626   Peter Minuit buys Manhattan Island from the Algonquin Indians

1664   New Amsterdam becomes New York when England gains control

1725   New York's first newspaper is published

1754   King's College (now Columbia University) is founded

1765   Stamp Act Congress meets in New York to protest unfair taxes

1775   Revolutionary War begins; George Washington sets up quarters in the city, but he and his troops are driven out of Manhattan by the British

1776   New York approves the Declaration of Independence

1783   Washington re-enters New York City in triumph

1785   New York City becomes first capital of the United States

1789   George Washington is inaugurated as first president of the United States

1812   The British blockade Manhattan in the War of 1812

1825   Erie Canal opens in upstate New York, linking New York City's Hudson River with the Great Lakes

1851   First edition of the *New York Times* is released

1861   The Civil War begins, with New York on the Union side

1871	Tammany Hall, a powerful political group in Manhattan, is temporarily put out of power
1883	The Brooklyn Bridge opens
1886	The Statue of Liberty is unveiled
1892	Ellis Island becomes a checkpoint for immigrants entering city
1902	Flatiron Building, New York's oldest skyscraper, is completed
1904	First subway goes into operation
1911	Triangle Shirtwaist Company fire kills 145 people and leads to new laws to protect workers
1920s	Harlem begins a time of growth in the arts
1929	Wall Street sees stock prices crash
1930	Chrysler building is completed
1931	The Empire State Building is completed
1939-40	New York is site for World's Fair, in Queens
1952	United Nations headquarters is completed
1964-65	New York hosts another World's Fair
1972	World Trade Center is completed
1983	Brooklyn Bridge centennial celebration
1986	Statue of Liberty centennial celebration
1988	The first New York International Festival of the Arts is held

Index